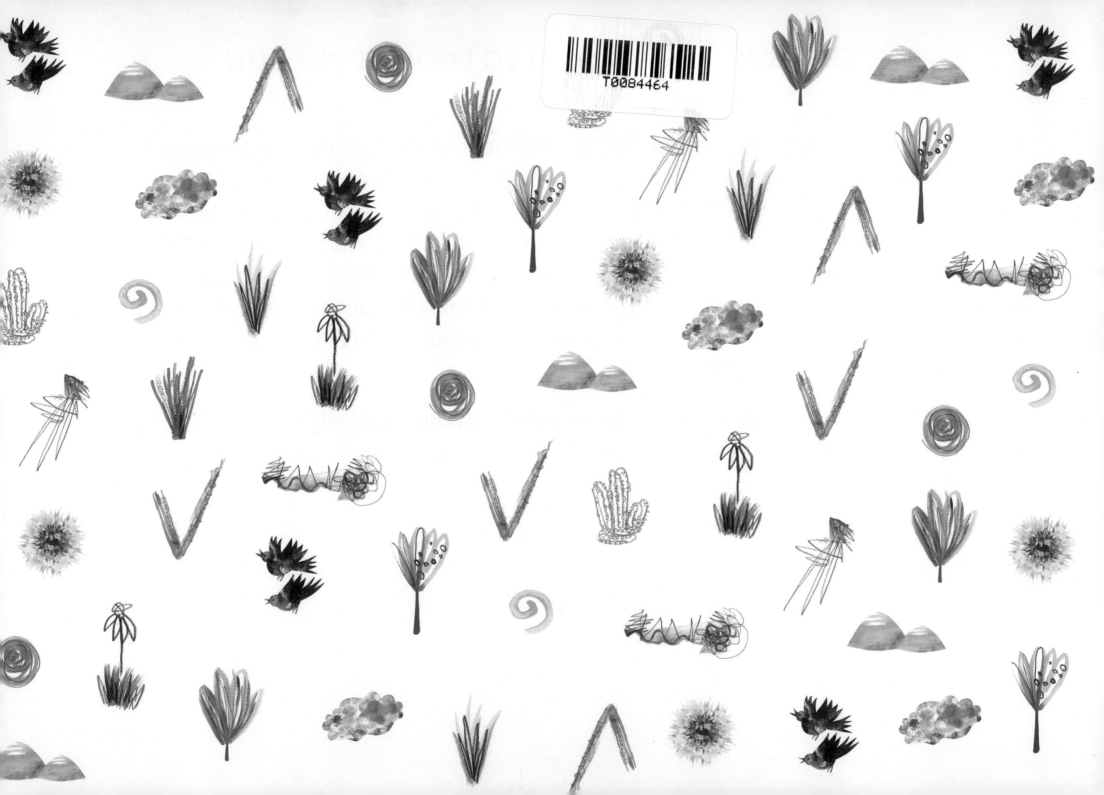

THE BOY WHO LONGED TO LOOK AT THE SUN

The Boy Who Longed to Look at the Sun is a therapeutic story about encouraging self-care. It tells the story of a boy who loves playing outside and becomes fixated with looking at the Sun, even though he has been warned it can hurt his eyes. Eventually the boy realises that his priorities have become skewed and he needs to look after his own well-being. The story teaches children the importance of looking after yourself and understanding what is or is not healthy. This beautifully illustrated storybook will appeal to all children, and can be used by practitioners, educators and parents as a tool to discuss the importance of well-being and self-care with children.

Juliette Ttofa is a Specialist Senior Educational Psychologist with 15 years' experience working with children and young people. She specialises in supporting resilience and well-being in vulnerable children.

Julia Gallego is a picture book illustrator and designer, and a graduate of the Manchester School of Art.

For my lovely Sandboy –

Devon

X

First published 2018 by Routledge
2 Park Square, Milton Park, Abingdon, Oxon OX14 4RN

52 Vanderbilt Avenue, New York, NY 10017

Routledge is an imprint of the Taylor & Francis Group, an informa business

British Library Cataloguing-in-Publication Data
A catalogue record for this book is available from the British Library
Library of Congress Cataloging-in-Publication Data
A catalog record for this title has been requested

ISBN: 978-1-138-30892-3 (pbk)
ISBN: 978-1-315-14321-7 (ebk)

Typeset in Calibri
by Apex CoVantage, LLC

The Boy Who Longed to Look at the Sun

A Story About Self-Care

Juliette Ttofa

Illustrated by Julia Gallego

Routledge
Taylor & Francis Group

LONDON AND NEW YORK

There was once a boy who loved to play in the sand.

Each sunny day he would go down to the beach to make

sand-castles, sand-boats and small pools for crabs to live in.

He was as happy as a sandboy.

1

Then one day, the Sun went in.

The clouds got bigger.

Then came the rain and the wind,

hail and thunder.

So the boy went inside, sad and disappointed.

But the boy longed to look at the Sun again so much that

he would spend hours and hours just staring into the sky.

He stared at the sky so much that he forgot all about playing.

And one day the Sun did come out again.

But the boy was so excited to see the Sun that he stared straight at it.

A grown-up warned him:

"Don't look directly at the Sun! It will hurt your eyes!"

The boy heard the grown up, but he was miserable and wanted cheering up, so he thought:

"How can it hurt my eyes? I can't feel a thing!"

So he kept looking, until the Sun hid behind the dark clouds once more and the boy became sad again.

3

Then a few days later, the Sun came out again and again the boy began to stare straight into its glare.

But it was so bright another grown-up exclaimed:

"Don't look directly at the Sun! You will get hurt!"

The boy listened, and tried to look away, but the temptation was too much, so he thought:

"I can't feel it hurting me.
What harm can it do?"

And he kept looking.

Until the day came when the Sun was going to be eclipsed by the Moon.

All the other children looked through special goggles to see it as the sky slid into darkness. Except the boy.

The sea-birds stopped singing.

The children whispered: "Don't look straight at the Sun! You will go blind!"

The boy listened, but try as he might to stop looking, he just could not do it, and he thought,

"It still isn't hurting me. Why does everyone keep saying that?"

The boy longed to see the Sun again so much that he could not look away.

Then a kind, wise person explained to him:

"You cannot feel pain in your eyes."

The boy realised that the Sun had been hurting him all along.
He just couldn't feel it through his eyes.

The boy finally shielded his eyes from the Sun.

He felt a deep, sudden pain in his heart:

"I have wanted to see
the Sun so much, that
I have not been thinking
straight," he sighed.

As the Sun's beams were revealed once more, the boy began to think more clearly....

He thought about all the warnings his friends had given him.

He thought about how he had ignored them and become blind to the truth.

"Perhaps I should listen to other people and learn to take care of myself."

So, one sunny morning the boy went down to the beach.

But this time, he put on some sunglasses and a hat.

And by and by, although he felt the warmth of the Sun's rays,

the boy learnt to look after himself

and began to look at life differently.

He began to play in the sand again.

He designed and crafted little pools decorated with beautiful rocks and shells for small sea creatures to play inside.

Other animals visited from far and wide to see the special habitats he would create.

And the boy stopped longing to look at the Sun.